Kai's Ancestral Shellmounds

by Angel Heart

POOR Press

ISBN 978-1-956534-09-2

Thank you to POOR Press team for design and copy-editing: Lisa "Tiny" Gray-Garcia, Maya Ram and A.S. Ikeda

**A POOR Press Publication © 2024 Angel Heart.
All Rights Reserved.**

POOR Press is a poor and indigenous people-led press dedicated to publishing the books and scholarship of youth, adults, and elders in poverty locally and globally.

**www.poormagazine.org
www.poorpress.net**

This book is dedicated to
My Guardian Angel Oya;
Warrior & Keeper of all entryways
into cemeteries & burial places.

Maferefun Oya!!

Introduction

In this third & final installment of a series by Author & Activist, Angel Heart; Kai discusses the ancestral shellmounds of his people, The Lisjan. With the permission of Corrina Gould, the Traditional Spokesperson for the Confederated Villages of Lisjan Nation, this book was created as part of a children's series.

HorŠe Tuuxi, My name is Kai!

Kai Talks About the Missions

Kai's Ancestral Shellmounds

"No Matter where you live in America, you're living on occupied land that Indigenous People were murdered for."

–Frank Waln

HorŠe Tuuxi! (Good Day) It's Kai! Today, I'm going to tell you all about Shellmounds. Do you know what a Shellmound is? Shellmounds are the burial sites or cemeteries of my ancestors.

My Lisjan ancestors are buried
in Shellmounds. Ancestors
are family that lived before us.
Ancestors are Great-Grandparents,
Grandmas, Grandpas, Aunties,
Uncles and Cousins.

When my peoples land was stolen by colonizers, they said that Shellmounds were middens, or trash heaps. Colonizers are people who came from Europe and stole First Nations Peoples land. Shellmounds are not trash heaps.

Shellmounds are made of shell, earth, and the bodies of my ancestors. We call Shellmounds our sacred burial sites because our loved ones are sacred to us. Sacred means someone, or something very special that deserves to be treated with respect.

Some Shellmounds were once so tall, they stood over 60 feet high and 600 feet wide! Some Shellmounds are over 5,000 years old. That's ancient! There's no Chochenyo word for Shellmound, because many words from our language were lost when we were enslaved by colonizers.

Not that long ago, greedy developers—people who wanted to build on top of places to make money—built a shopping mall on top of our Shellmounds. My people asked them not to. We explained that our burial sites are sacred. Destroying our sacred places also destroys our history and our people.

Even when the greedy developers found and removed hundreds of my ancestors bones, they built on top of them anyway. Greedy Developers ignored us and desecrated what is sacred. People shopping at the Bay Street Mall in Emeryville, California, don't know that all of my ancestors remains weren't removed, and that they are shopping on top of my ancestors bodies.

That's how colonizers were able to build on top of my ancestors, because everybody believed the lie of colonizers calling our shellmounds piles of trash. . Colonization has brought much harm to our ancestors and is still bringing harm to our people today.

One way that my Grandma taught people and the public about our burials, was to hold a Shellmound Peace Walk in 2005. All of our family, friends and supporters showed up to walk with us. Each walk took people to a different Shellmound, where we prayed for each sacred site, and for the ancestors who are buried there.

Folks can stand-up and help my people by giving us our land back. They can also support us by coming to the Shellmound protest in Emeryville. We gather there on the day-after, what is now called, Thanksgiving (but we call it ThangsTaken).

This day is the biggest shopping day of the year, and every year we all meet, and come together with our friends, allies and community. Together, we let shoppers know that the mall is on top of our ancestors sacred burial site.

My Grandma would like everyone to know that "the West Berkeley Shellmound is the oldest of our 425 plus sacred sites in the Bay Area, and that we need continuous support. Shellmounds deserve to be preserved and protected."

Our shellmounds were placed on the endangered list by the National Historic Preservation Organization in 2020. My Grandma says, "Our family and Tribes have come to our shellmounds for hundreds & thousands of years to pray; and that we deserve a place to do that still."

My Grandma says, "That's her blessing. It's her grandchildren's blessing to be born on the land that our ancestors have always lived and been on." My Grandma works hard everyday to teach people about the land they live and walk on. I'm Kai. I'm Lisjan and my ancestors are sacred!

Glossary

Allies - those who are cooperating with one another for a similar purpose

Ancestor - a person who one is descended from, more remote than a grandparent

Ancient - belonging to the very distant past

Bay Area - a region of California based around the San Francisco bay

Blessing - a prayer; gift or favor given by God, the Creator, or the Great Spirit

Burial - a ceremony in which a body is given a funeral and grave

Cemetery - a burial ground or graveyard

Chochenyo - original language spoken in the East Bay Area of what is now referred to as California

Colonizer - a country that sends settlers to steal land and resources from places that are not theirs

Community - a group of people living in the same place with shared resources

Continuous - forming an unbreakable whole with no interruption

Cremated - to dispose of a dead person's body by burning it to ashes

Desecrated - to have treated a sacred place with violent disrespect

Destroy - to put an end to the existence of something by damaging or attacking it; to ruin spiritually or emotionally

Developers - a person or thing that causes something to spread or expand

Disrespect - a lack of respect or courtesy; to insult

Endangered - at serious risk of extinction

Enslaved - to have been made a slave; to have made someone a slave

Europe - a continent of the Eastern and Northern Hemisphere

First Nations - any of the groups of Indigenous peoples of the Americas; including Canada, North American, Central America and South America

Greedy - having or showing an intense and selfish desire for something; including wealth and power

Historic - important in history

HorSe' Tuuxi - Chochenyo word meaning good day

Ignore - to refuse to acknowledge; to disregard

Indigenous - to originate from a particular place; native

Insult - to treat with disrespect

Interred - to place in a grave

Lisjan - a nation of Ohlone peoples

Midden - a heap of trash

Nation - a large group of people united by common descent, history, culture or language

National - relating to a nation

Native - a person born to a specified place or land

Occupied - being used or taken up by someone

Ohlone - a member of a group or nation of Indigenous People, who live in the coastal areas of California

Peace - freedom from disturbance; tranquility

Prayed - to have made a solemn statement, request, statement, or to give thanks to God, the Creator or the Great Spirit

Preservation - the act of preserving something

Preserved/Preserving - to maintain something in its original or current state

Protected - preserved from harm; especially by formal or legal measures

Protest - a statement or action expressing disapproval of something

Remains - the dead body of human; cremated or otherwise

Resources - a source or supply of something

Respect - a feeling of deep admiration for someone or something; regard for the feelings, rights and traditions of others

Sacred - dedicated to God, the Creator, or the Great Spirit; dedicated to a religion or spiritual path

Settler - a person who invades; someone who steals or uses land and resources that do not belong to them

Shellmound - sacred burial site of the Lisjan Nation; and Ohlone peoples

Site - an area of land or ground

Society - a community of people living together; an organization or club formed for a particular purpose or activity

Support - to bear the weight or hold; to give assistance to

Supporters - a person or people who approve of and encourages someone or something

Photo Credits

Cover Image: 1926 Shellmound Desecration Photograph by The City of Emeryville

Frank Wahn Quote: Land Back Flag at Homefulness/POOR Magazine

Page 8: Kai at DeeColonize Academy Graduation by Deja Gould

Page 9: Recreated image of Indigenous "Californians" fishing in tule canoe by sanjosehistory.org/pre-history

Page 10: Kids Against Colonialism art work by Save the West Berkeley Shellmound

Page 11: Shells & Earth Photo by Public Domain Photos/Stock Image

Page 12: 1926 Shellmound Desecration by The City of Emeryville

Page 13: Protect Ohlone Sacred Sites art by The West Berkeley Shellmound

Page 14: 1902 Shellmound Desecration & Demolishing by The Bay Street Mall in Emeryville, CA

Page 15: Historically NOT Private Property, Colonialism IS Trespassing protest sign by Save the West Berkeley Shellmound

Page 16: 2005 Shellmound Peace Walk by protectsogoreate.org

Page 17: Save West Berkeley Shellmound Mural by Save the West Berkeley Shellmound

Page 18: Shellmound Protest titled Shellmound to Shellmound,

Emeryville, CA by Save the West Berkeley Shellmound

Page 19: Corrina Gould speaking at the West Berkeley Shellmound by Save the West Berkeley Shellmound

Page 20: West Berkeley Shellmound non-violent direct action by Save the West Berkeley Shellmound

Page 21: Corrina Gould with her Granddaughter by Save the West Berkeley Shellmound

Acknowledgements & Website

I would like to acknowledge and thank Kai, Deja, and Corrina Gould for the blessing of being permitted to write this book. Their family is an inspiration to many. I'm grateful for their teachings about sacred shellmound burial sites, and all of the information they share, about ways in which we can continue to support them. Profits/Proceeds from the purchase of this book benefits the Sogorea Te Land Trust. **www.sogoreate-landtrust.org**

I would also like to thank POOR Press, Lisa "Tiny" Gray-Garcia, Muteado Silencio, A.S. Ikeda ,and Maya Ram for their leadership, instruction, facilitation and copy editing of this book. I'm grateful for the entire POOR Magazine Family. A BIG THANK YOU to the POOR Magazine Solidarity Family & Bank of ComeUnity Reparations for making this book possible.

Angel Heart, Quechua-Puna, is an Activist, Author, Poverty Scholar & Homefulness Resident. She is currently leading a project and radio show with POOR Magazine on 96.1 FM - PNN-KEXU titled, "The Peoples Botanica."

Angel Heart is an Intuitive-Empath with many years of knowledge & practice in Espiritismo & Brujeria. She provides spiritual readings, or consultas, and is the creator of The People's Botanica - A Spiritual Wellness & Supplies Market.

www.ingramcontent.com/pod-product-compliance
Lightning Source LLC
Chambersburg PA
CBHW041527090426
42736CB00035B/39